come as you are

the art of unbecoming who they told *you* to be

jessica **burgio**

Come As You Are: The Art of Unbecoming Who They Told You to Be

ISBN 979-8-9870447-4-2 (paperback)
ISBN 979-8-9870447-3-5 (eBook)

Editing & Layout: Megs Thompson — megswrites llc

www.inomniaparatuspublishing.com

This book is dedicated to you!

To helping you realize you're not stuck with the cards you've been dealt. If you're reading this book, it's *for you.* You might be thinking how is it for *me?* While you may not be the only one to read this book, I wrote it **for** you because I was you. And there's still many parts of me that are still you. Our healing journey and our journey of self-discovery is not linear.

I hope you find yourself in my story as you read along. And I pray you start to deeply understand how powerful you truly are. That you are the leader of your destiny, that you DO have a choice and a say in how you show up in this world. The art of unbecoming who they told you to be is my perspective gift to you… I hope it brings us closer. I hope you see you probably aren't to far away from the life you desire.

Small daily habits can create massive change in your life, creating your non-negotiables, and deciding what boundaries to enforce will shape your life, supporting you in unbecoming who 'they' told you to be.

Freeing yourself from the comparisons of life, the limitations of circumstance, and '*starting to believe in yourself a little more than you don't,*' (one of my favorite Jenn Gottlieb quotes) will shape your destiny…

Who you become in the process is the exciting part right?! The possibilities of stepping into your true potential power are limitless. I get chills even writing this to you. I see you. I honor you. And I'm with you. It's an absolute honor to share this experience WITH you. So thank you for spending time with me, and I'd love if you continue hanging with me. You can do that through the podcast. We can hang out every week! Yay!

Again, sending you so much love. Honor the place you are in and then DECIDE what needs to happen in order to start. You don't have to know exactly where you are going or how you'll get there today... just figure out the NEXT RIGHT STEP. (This always helps take the overwhelm out of it for me)

Your biggest cheerleader

Jess

Table of Contents

Foreword

As I read through the manuscript of this book it became clear that almost everything I knew growing up, I knew because of my older sister.

Jessica always did what she wanted. As her little brother, she made me realize I wasn't wrong for being rebellious. She, like me, had seen the reality of life and realized that the suffering of going against your true self was far worse than the suffering of going against society's "rules."

Going through these pages taught me many new things about my sister, and even more about myself.

One important thing Jessica teaches us is how indecision and fear are the disease of life, and calculated action is the cure. My favorite chapter is "Indecisive No More" where she helps guide us through how we can make more practical decisions in times where we may be feeling emotional or overwhelmed.

Using her natural ability to make new friends, bring people together, inspire others, develop and maintain successful businesses, remain grounded, and stay in shape, through these pages, Jess encourages each of us to do the same, and to stop letting others tell us who to be.

- Dominic Aljundi

Jessica Burgio

Introduction

Writing this book has been a labor of love. A project I've wanted to take on for no less than 20 years, but always knew that for whatever reason, the timing wasn't right, not yet. But now, as I celebrate my 41st rotation around the sun, I know with confidence that it's time. This book is my gift to you. My fellow accidental entrepreneurs, beauty professionals, and creative badasses who've spent far too many years following the rules and doing exactly what you were told to.

No matter who you are or where you're from, the unspoken 'rules' of the world tell us we're expected to go to school, earn a degree, land a job, get married, buy a house, have kids, pay bills, work until we physically can't, retire, and die. We're conditioned to believe without hesitation that following this outline will somehow set us up for living a successful life. While there are some individuals who find great joy and fulfillment by checking these boxes, I can tell you right now, I'm not one of them. And, if you've picked up this book, I'm guessing you aren't either.

I sometimes wonder, how my life might have shaped up differently, if only I'd been taught that it was okay to ask for help. For one thing, I know it wouldn't have been as lonely or messy as it got at times, but we also probably wouldn't be sharing this moment right now. If I had all the secrets, all the answers, I sure as fuck would just make a list and send it out to the world, sadly, life doesn't work like that. If it did, the practice of personal development wouldn't exist, there would be no need for therapists or coaches, and no one would ever feel the sadness and desperation that I did, in my darkest days. But they also wouldn't experience the elation and fulfillment I have now, having come through the darkness and feeling the badass San Diego sun on my upturned face.

I've known my whole life that words have power. From the moment I was first told to be quiet. To stop acting 'like that.' To dampen the sassy, loud, brash, and unfiltered girl I was, I tried desperately to fit in and be 'normal.' I tried to shut her up for so many years, fighting to fit in and be like 'them.' The smart girls, so fit and pretty, and pleasing. But I'm average, chunky, a smartass, and anything but normal. Out of my desperation to be accepted, I found myself setting out to 'do all the things' that a girl like me should do. I spent years, unfulfilled, focused only on checking the boxes of the things I was told I should want. The things I was told I should do. The person I was told I should be.

I went to school. I got the job. I found a career I was really, really good at. I made the money. I met the right people. I got married. But it wasn't until I fell in love again, true love, that I could actually begin to trust my own inner voice, instead of those around me. She'd been trying to talk to me for so long, and I'd gotten really good at ignoring her. Locking her away in a gilded cage while I focused on the next big thing. The next box I needed to check.

If I could give you only one piece of advice, it would be to stop distracting yourself. That's it. Only once you've cleared away the distractions that are keeping your attention from what matters most, will you make room for the magic you hold but have been too busy to see.

Trapped safely in my seat, flying at 10,000 feet, I sit with my thoughts, able to pause and see things so much more clearly than I can with my feet on the ground. I'm able to recognize the emotions and thoughts that need to be felt and acknowledged. I've been flying almost weekly for the better part of the last five years, between visiting a client who lives in the Bay Area, and now, to spend time a man who's swept me off my feet. In these few hours of quiet space, when I find myself alone amongst a crowded flight, I've been able to dig deeper into who I am, and who I want to be, as a mom and a business owner, a coach, and a hairstylist. In the past, I've always prioritized thoughts about the needs of my family or my clients before my own, haunted by an overwhelming to do list that seems to grow longer by the day.

Growing up, I watched my mom hustling, working early, late, and on weekends, sending us to the babysitter's so she could build her own business. After having me at only 19, she did what she had to, and I have the utmost respect for my mom. She's always lived life on her own terms and succeeded in creating a million-dollar business within a market that wasn't yet operating anywhere near that level. My mom is a mother fucking boss in her own right, self-taught, self-motivated, and self-driven. She's my greatest mentor, as well as the person I blame for my own conditioned behavior of constantly needing to prove my worth. While I know she never intended to teach me such unrealistic behavioral patterns, watching her, I learned early that if you want something done right you have to do it yourself. As we've both gotten older, we've grown closer, as adults, as women, as badass business owners. I've learned the importance of setting healthy boundaries and understand that we're all doing the best we can with what we know at the time. I know now that the reason my mom pushed me the way she did, was because she wanted more for me than was possible for her.

So, let's dig right in. I believe that one of the biggest factors when it comes to creating and living a successful life, is first defining specifically what success means to us personally. This is something I work through with many of my clients, and a topic that they often choose to revisit, because as our lives change, so do the things that we place the highest level of importance and value on.

Let's try something really quick. Take just a moment and think back to the first person you dated, the first job you worked, or any other possibly horrible decision you made that at the time, you thought was the absolute bees-knees. It's probably fair to say your values, choices, and definition of success have changed a bit since then. I know mine have! Sure, there was a point in my life when I thought having a baby with a devil-may-care, party boy was the best idea. *Spoiler: While it may not have been the best idea, it has, without a doubt, had the best ROI. My son is the light of my life and the why behind my personal definition of success.* I smoked for years, because it's what everyone else was doing, and working in the beauty industry, smoking was often the only time we would get a break all day. Again, not the best decision.

Needless to say, my priorities, values, and idea of success have evolved as I've grown up, experienced life, and further explored who I am, but still, I found myself having spent 20-years in a career that from all outward appearances was massively successful, yet completely unfulfilling. I did everything I was supposed to, and nothing that I wasn't. I followed the rules, striving to meet the expectations set for me by others, achieving success by their standards but realizing that the life I'd created wasn't one that felt successful to me. I had hit all the milestones, done all the things, and still I was moving through every day feeling unfulfilled, exhausted, and lost - because I'd never given myself a chance to explore what success meant to me.

Like so many of you, I bought into the lies that society feeds us. That everyone has a job they dislike, you just have to stick it out because (*I hate this line btw*) 'that's why they call it work.' That if you get married and are miserable, you just have to deal with it, because you both made a decision and are now stuck with the repercussions. Our world is full of creative entrepreneurs that are sick and tired of trying to fit into a box that other people are shoving them in - scared shitless to show up authentically and put themselves out there.

Now, before we get too much further, this book is not for everyone. However, if you've read this far, you know that already. This book is for 'us.' The people who've always felt like they knew they were meant for more. The people who've looked around themselves and thought, 'this can't be it.' This book is for those of us who did what we were told, followed the rules, and checked the boxes, only to realize again and again that something wasn't right.

My goal, in writing this book, is that you recognize the areas in your life where you may not be feeling fulfilled and see them as not as a prison sentence but an opportunity for self-discovery and exploration. The way we learn anything in life is through trial and error, it's not often that we get things right on the first try, and even then, there are lessons we can learn about ourselves, our passions, our desires, and our own personal definitions of what it means to live a successful life.

It's time for a change - Let's do this!

Confidence isn't something you have. It's something you work on building every single day.

How It Started

When I was 17 and a junior in high school, my best friend convinced me it would be a good idea to attend beauty school together after graduation. With the help of financial aid, it was basically free, so while my mom was dead set against it, she couldn't really say no. I was already working part time as a waitress and had my own car, so I felt like an adult, and decided, as most 17-year-old's will, to do what I wanted. For three months, I followed along with the lessons, but hated every minute of it. I quit before I had a chance to even touch a real head of hair.

Because I was still living at home with my mom, I committed to her that I'd enroll at our local community college and pursue a degree — to make something of myself. When I planned my first quarter, I was excited to sign up for college level English courses. The only class I'd ever enjoyed in school was English because I could express myself with no judgment, and I looked forward to being able to spend time developing and honing skills that I already felt quite confident in. Sadly, my naive dreams were killed when I realized that the straight A's I'd gotten in high school English didn't actually mean I knew anything at all.

College level English kicked my ass and was a reality slap. Not only did I get a D in my first class, but when I stubbornly signed up to retake the course with the same professor the following quarter, I wound up with an F! It was then that I realized I'm not someone who learns in traditional ways. I need to be shown examples and allowed to get my hands dirty. I'm definitely a trial-and-error kinda gal! So, I quit community college too.

Throwing caution to the wind, I spent a year traveling, working temporary restaurant jobs, and eventually meandered my way back home. By that time, my best friend had graduated from beauty school, was working in a salon, and loving every moment of it. She urged me to give it another try, especially since the hours I'd already earned were only good for a few more months, otherwise, I'd have to start over from scratch. The only issue was that this time, I'd have to pay tuition. $8,000, which at the time, I definitely didn't have.

Not only did I have to take out a loan to cover my tuition, but I had to beg my mom to let me move back in and live at home rent free. I still remember drafting a handwritten contract, guaranteeing that not only would I be attending beauty school, but I'd be applying to work at the best salon in San Diego as soon as I graduated.

It's true what they say that we take things more seriously when we've got skin in the game. This time, I attended classes, dedicated myself fully to learning everything I could, and graduated top five of the class, all while happily charging $6 for roller sets and perfecting the art of pedicures on seventy-year-old men.

A year later, fresh out of beauty school, I started my career at Robert Cromeans salon, the best salon in San Diego, just like I'd promised mom. At the time the salon had 45 stylists and 15 assistants. It was massive, overwhelming, scary, and I quickly learned that I didn't know shit about what it meant to start at the bottom. I was a toilet scrubber, an errand girl, and the only hair I touched was on the floor or in a shampoo bowl. Talk about a quick ego check. But throughout those months of hell, I also knew that I had found my people. The level of authenticity in that building was next level, even if we were all just trying to be cooler than each other. I can still remember walking into the salon for the first time and seeing a room full of freaks. Vibrantly colored hair, black clothes, tattoos, and piercings — it was like looking in a mirror and I thought for the first time, *'It's okay to be me. I get to be weird! This is where I belong!'*

That first year I learned how to be a hairdresser, and what clients really want. I learned how to tailor conversations to each unique guest and started to understand the importance of holding space for someone else, even if it was only temporarily while giving them a trim, touch up, or blow out. This was when I realized that to be a successful stylist, my priority needed to be the conversation, experience, and time shared with my clients. Their hair was secondary. This is also when I first learned what it means to unapologetically show up as whoever the fuck you want it to be — and I was hooked. I was driving half an hour to work every day, scrubbing toilets and color bowls, living off peanut butter and jelly sandwiches, and was the happiest I'd ever been. Those were the days when you only got a break if you smoked, so I started stealing cigarettes from girl's pockets in the coat room, because it meant time spent outside with my new tribe.

Looking back, even though the intent of the stylists during that first year was to break us, talking shit about how we dressed, looked, smelled, laughed. They also taught us the foundations of what it means to have a successful profession in the beauty industry. You don't show up to work looking like you're hungover, even if you feel like you've been hit by a city bus. You put your fucking face on, get your nails done, and when you have time off, you go do things in the world so that when you interact with clients, you can hold thoughtful and entertaining conversations. There's nothing worse than a boring stylist. When you're behind the chair, your clients need to find you interesting, so that even if you're not the best technical hairdresser, you're still the most captivating person they know.

I was worried, like really worried, because everyone around me ate, slept, and breathed hair. It was all they talked about. Every weekend they were attending a different hair show or training event. I thought for sure that I was doomed, because while I loved hair, I loved a lot of other things too, and enjoyed spending my spare time on those hobbies, since hair had become my career. About this time, I started getting into weightlifting, fitness, and really taking better care of my body. I stopped smoking cigarettes. Paid better attention to my diet, and before I knew it, I started noticing that my clients at the salon, were becoming personal training clients as well. Without knowing it, I was magnetizing the right people for me, my personality, my skills, and expertise. Looking back now, I also realize that this was also my first foray into coaching others, while I definitely didn't realize it at the time.

Robert Cromeans had a vision for his salon and knew without hesitation how he wanted things to happen. He was the first person I'd interacted with who took their career so seriously but was also doing it his own crazy way. This was years ago, and he was already charging $500 an hour, weird leather pants, extravagant hats, and dead animals as a belt. He was the coolest person I'd ever met, and whether he knew it or not, he showed me then, what was possible.

After just over a year as an assistant, I was presented with an unbelievable opportunity to join two long-time stylists as their right-hand gal, in a new salon they were opening. I saw this as a chance to prove mom wrong. I was going to make 6-figures, I was going to be successful, and I was going to do it my way. I was 22 years old and knew jack shit about leadership. Hell, I barely knew how to cut hair.

Over the next three years, I learned some pretty invaluable lessons about life, choices, business, and love. I learned the hard way that many people have visions and dreams but lack the ability to integrate and implement those to become a reality. I learned that there is no such thing as a 'one man show.' That it takes a team to develop a vision from a hobby into a business. Before long, the new salon wasn't doing well. Checks were bouncing, and while I was personally able to grow a six-figure clientele through networking and good old-fashioned hustling in only six months, the salon itself wasn't stable.

A big lesson I learned early on in my career was that confidence isn't something you have. It's something you work on building every single day.

I started pushing myself out of my comfort zone more and more, saying yes to opportunities that scared me, testing my own limits, and realizing that with every experience, not only did I not die, but my confidence was growing by leaps and bounds. Before long I was being asked to teach other stylists, sometimes in salons, other times on stages at hair shows and events. I found myself being flown all over the country to learn techniques and experiment with products from big names like Bumble and Bumble.

In a snap, the first 10-years of my career were over, and they'd flown by in a heartbeat. I was living the hairdresser life, moving at the speed of light, pedal to the metal, with absolutely zero personal life, because there simply isn't time. I'd bought my first house at 22, complete with a mortgage I most definitely couldn't afford, and had gotten married at 25 to someone who was still figuring out what they wanted in life. Our marriage was doomed to fail because I already knew who I was and what I wanted, and the way I saw it, he just couldn't keep up. I'd get home after a really busy day at work, not wanting to have to interact with anyone, or be a member of our team. After two years it became blindingly obvious that we didn't really know each other at all and weren't right for each other. At least not at the time. Looking back, if we'd both made more of an effort from the start, we probably could have figured out a way for things to work.

Then I lost my mind for about a year when I was 27. I got divorced, sold my house, and moved to the beach. My ex took one dog, and I kept the other. I started getting back into weightlifting, because it allowed me to feel like I had control over something, even if that something was just my own body. I won the first show I ever competed in, and the feeling of being the best at something, proving to myself and others that I was a winner, reignited a belief that I could do anything I put my mind to. I knew that my physique wasn't the best, but because I'd grown up as a gymnast, a cheerleader, and a performer, I was able to outperform everyone else on stage. Proof again that you don't have to be the best technically skilled person in the room, but if you can bring the whole package, leaning into your strengths and not obsessing about your weaknesses, quite often, you'll be the most memorable.

I was devastated when my trainer at the time, a dear friend, informed me that she wouldn't be able to continue coaching me. At the time, I thought she was jealous, that she was afraid I was going to be better than she was. In reality, she could see then what I couldn't, that the path I was on wasn't a healthy one.

Get out there and find the best coach that you can. Make the investment. Do what they tell you and show up every single day.

While training, I'd started dating someone new. He was a happy go lucky party guy, and we always had a lot of fun when we were together, connecting in a way I hadn't with anyone else. We'd both experienced our fair share of shitty relationships and were glad to have found a friendship, a partnership, in each other. We were lying in bed one evening and made the decision that we wanted to have a baby. He was going out of town, and I had my weightlifting competition, but we agreed that after he returned, and my competition was done, we'd talk about giving it a try. Six weeks later I was pregnant.

Becoming a mom has been the craziest, most pivotal experience of my life. It's exciting, terrifying, and exhilarating all at once. The realization that everything I'd been working for, training for, it was all going to change. Getting up early to train at the gym before rushing to the salon for back-to-back clients all day. Making $150,000 a year. Working hard and loving it. None of that mattered anymore. Having a kid, becoming a mom, you realize pretty quickly that your life, isn't about you anymore.

My son, Kai, has been the biggest blessing I've ever received. He's taught me love, compassion, and patience. Patience with myself. Patience with my career. Patience with others. Patience with knowing I want to do big things and trusting that they'll happen when the time is right. One of the biggest reasons for why I waited until I was 30 to have a baby was because I knew that I wanted to be able to shift my career around so that I could be off in the evenings and the weekends. Spending that time with my son is the priority, and my career needed to fit around him. I know there are plenty of hairdressers who have amazing careers, working only the hours they choose, never sacrificing their weekends or evenings, and that's great! But for me, I knew that I wanted different. I wanted to find a way to stop trading my time for money, and that's when I really started exploring my options.

Ask yourself:

What do I love doing more than anything else?

Now, how can you put more of THAT in your daily life?

What Got You Here Won't Get You There

Looking back now, it seems like immediately after I made the decision to start exploring what other options I might have, I was approached with offers to do editorial pieces and magazine work. During one of those gigs, I met the owner of Strong Fitness Magazine, a great guy who's become an amazing mentor and friend. After connecting once or twice, he started inviting me along on some of his different photography shoots. Spending time behind the scenes on set gave me the opportunity to do something I'd always dreamt of styling and pampering models for professional magazine shoots. It also piqued my curiosity about what it takes to be a model, and how it was these gorgeous, athletic women were chosen to be featured in the magazine.

It was then that I learned another big secret to getting ahead in life and business. Ask for what you want. I couldn't believe it was that easy, but I informed him right then and there that I was going to work my ass off, get back into really good shape, and he'd be hearing from me soon, asking to be featured in a future issue. Sure enough, six weeks later I was flying up to Canada and shooting for a full four-page spread in Strong Fitness Magazine.

Around the same time, I had the pleasure of meeting Lori Harder, an unbelievably powerful author, speaker, cover model, and three-time fitness world champion. We became fast friends, and she was kind enough to invite me to attend her newest creative venture, The Bliss Project. To say I was overwhelmed would be an understatement. I was surrounded by a room full of woman, strangers, all crying and connecting like they'd met each other years before, not hours. I was shocked and uncomfortable. I already had friends. I didn't need to be here. It was intimidating and a complete sensory overload, but at the end of the retreat, I begged Lori to let me come back the following year as a volunteer. Yes, I was scared and uncomfortable, but I knew that I needed to feel that energy again.

I started exploring more and more, everything I could about personal development, the different modalities, practices, and methods. Until that point, I had read all of the books, listened to the podcasts, and I genuinely thought I was doing the work, but I soon realized that in actuality I was only adjusting, moving things around in my life. I wasn't actually doing the work, at least not yet. I still needed to learn how to go about integrating the things I was learning about myself into my life. I needed to hit rock bottom and realize that what I was doing wasn't working anymore and give myself permission to want more.

One of my favorite sayings is what got you here won't get you there. If you want to stay where you are, doing what you're doing, that's okay. But if you want different, you've got to do different, you've got to make different decisions.

After my first year attending Lori's Bliss Project Retreat, I started seeking out ways to put myself in more and more uncomfortable situations where I was open and vulnerable to whatever might happen. I met incredible people who were in similar phases of life. I made a point of reaching out via social media and saying hello to people that I would have previously felt weird or intimidated about approaching. Little did I know, this new method of networking online was going to have unbelievable impacts on both my life and business. By 'connecting' or becoming 'friends' with people online, I was able to meet and interact with their friends, expanding my own circle with individuals who were seeking the same things I was. During this time, I connected with so many phenomenal people who've gone on to become my tribe, my cheerleaders, my colleagues, resources, inspiration, and mentees.

I was able to watch as other people were doing the things I'd long been dreaming of, inspiring me to take action myself when in the past I may have waited forever, never actually doing the thing. For example, I'd been saying I wanted to start a podcast for years, but never did. Then, I watched as Lori launched her podcast, hitting first 5, then 10-million downloads. It was wild, seeing what she was accomplishing, all because she made the decision to start.

Through Lori, I met her husband, Chris, the genius behind the Fast Foundations Mastermind, an early-stage entrepreneur mastermind group developed specifically for people looking to grow or scale their businesses online. Because of the connections I'd already made with both Lori and Chris I knew without hesitation, I wanted to be involved in the Fast Foundations mastermind but wasn't sure if I'd qualify to participate because at the time, my business was brick and mortar. I was a beauty professional and hair stylist. My business was based solely on my being behind a chair, but something told me to reach out. So, I did it. I asked for what I wanted. I sent both Lori and Chris a DM, saying, *"Hey, I see you have this awesome mastermind for early-stage entrepreneurs, and I want in, but it says it's only for online folks, is there any chance you'd make an exception?"* Chris responded right away letting me know that of course I was welcome, telling me that the group was designed for anyone who identified as an accidental entrepreneur — still one of my absolute favorite titles.

I genuinely believe that every creative artist, beauty professional, and trend-setter is in their own way, an accidental entrepreneur. While our business, industry, and services may vary, we all possess the same deep desire to pave our own path and do things the way we believe they should be done. We crave the creative freedom to make choices based on what feels right to us, following our intuition and honoring who we are at our core.

I don't think I could have whipped out my credit card any faster. Sure, it was scary, dropping $8,000 on something brand new to me, but I was ready to make that investment in myself, and my future. I attended that first mastermind in February of 2019, with the hope that I'd meet a few new friends, interacting and learning from 50 likeminded accidental entrepreneurs who were looking to make changes in their own lives and may even be able to help me figure out what the best next steps might be for me. I walked into the room and was overcome with emotions. We were each called to the front of the room to introduce ourselves ("hot seats" as we call them now). Easy, right? Wrong! As I waited for my turn, I had every intention of standing up and saying, *"Hey, my name's Jess and I'm done with hair. FUCK HAIR! I don't want to be a part of this community anymore."* Sure, I'd hit 6-figues, doing hair, but I still never felt like it was enough, like I could call hairdressing a real career. But then, when it was my turn, and I looked out at the faces of these people who were so eager to hold space for me, lift me up, and learn with me, I knew I needed to go back to the industry that had raised me and help the people who were just starting out. I wanted to be that voice of encouragement and empowerment that the past version of Jess needed.

We can get passionate about a lot of different things, but passion is different than purpose.

At the time, I was at the top of my game, making well over 6-figures a year traveling constantly to meet with out-of-town clients and working on magazine shoots. I think throughout our lives, we serve different purposes. We may feel like we're meant to be doing one thing for years, but then wake up one day and realize, it's not the right focus for us any longer. I knew after attending my first mastermind that I'd touched as many people as I could through my work as a hairdresser, and I felt a pull to step out from behind the chair, sharing the lessons I've learned, the struggles I've faced, and encouraging my fellow accidental entrepreneurs and beauty professionals to push through imposter syndrome and spread the light of their own message, whatever the fuck that message might be. Of course, it wasn't my time, at least not yet.

Entrepreneurship is a lot like raising a kid. Just when they start crawling, and you get used to that, baby proofing your entire world at ground level, they start walking and you have to go back to square one. Then they switch it up on you, right? They stop crying, and sleep through the night, then suddenly, they won't sleep at all.

That's life though. We figure one thing out and then life throws us a curveball. Speaking of curveballs…

After 15 years of waiting to find the perfect space, I signed a lease on my own salon 6-months before the world was rocked by the COVID-19 Pandemic in March of 2020. One of my longtime clients had come in for an appointment and was randomly mentioned that a loft next door to their office was coming available. Right there in downtown San Diego, next door to the ballpark in a second story loft, situated between two amazing restaurants. I pressed him for more details, and when he got back to the office later that afternoon, he sent over a quick video walk-through of the space, I made an appointment to see it in person, and 6 weeks later I had my own salon. The owner of the building was amazing, they gave me a killer deal, a great lease, and they had a contractor ready to make any necessary changes to turn what had been an office into my dream five chair salon.

When we left the Fast Foundations Mastermind, we were each presented with a challenge, to return home and start something new. It could be anything, so long as it lit us up, and encouraged us to further explore our own passions and purpose. I had the idea of creating a networking group for hairdressers. It seemed that for many of us, the only time we got together with other professionals was to learn new techniques, things that would benefit our clients, but I wanted to create something different. A way for beauty professionals to hang out and do something for our own personal development and growth. That was my first experience sharing and teaching the things I'd learned at the mastermind, and it was amazing.

25 people attended my first event. I had lined up speakers, food, vendors, and a DJ. Looking back now, I realize that I asked other people to attend as speakers because I was too scared to position myself as being the main presenter. I wasn't ready for others to see me as an expert because I didn't see myself that way, not yet. Everyone that attended had amazing things to say about the event, and I went on to host a few more events, at a friend's salon, and then, in October 2019, at my own! The topics ranged from goal setting, non-negotiables, reverse engineering your income, and maintaining a work/life balance. Life was good, business was thriving. Then the pandemic hit, and we were forced to close our doors. Like everyone else around the world, I was at a loss as far as how to proceed.

One afternoon, I caught a snippet of our governor here in California talking about how people could still work outside while socially distancing and staying safe. When I looked out the window, I knew there was no way in hell that would work for salons the way it did for restaurants. I knew what these closures were doing for beauty professionals, and I wanted to give a voice to our industry. This was the first time I knew that I could make a difference. So, I finally started that podcast. I had a client who was a phenomenal videographer, and he agreed to meet me at the salon, since it was closed, to record audio and video for the first 25 episodes. I called it Beauty Inspires Beauty and set out to have thought-provoking conversations about the beauty industry, talking with other professionals about how they got from where they were to where they are now. .

I quickly realized how expensive things were going to get, if I continued having every episode professionally recorded for video, especially when I didn't yet know how I was planning to market or monetize this new adventure. So, I started using the process I still use today, recording conversations via Zoom, and streaming those online, while having the audio edited and loaded onto the many different audio streaming platforms. For the first 6 months, I was recording one episode a week, then moved up to two episodes weekly, and as of the writing of this book, I've brought on another badass hairdresser as a cohost and we're recording three episodes every week. The goal is still to have amazing, thought-provoking conversations around life and business from a wide variety of creative, accidental entrepreneurs. Talking about where they've come from, and how unbecoming what they were told they should be, has allowed them to pursue their own purpose. I want people to understand that you can shift out of stuff, your current situation doesn't have to be a life sentence, but no one else is going to make that decision for you.

If I'm not at least a little *scared* about something, it probably means I don't care.

Don't Let Fear Hold You Back

One of my favorite things about having my own podcast, is getting to interview and chat with whoever I want, about whatever I want. I know that my audience is comprised of my people. So, when I get excited about something or someone, it's a pretty solid bet that they will too. Earlier this year I sat down to record an impromptu episode (as I often do) and thought it might be fun to have my 10-year-old son Kai join me, as a special guest.

Of course, when I asked him what he thought about the idea, his response was typical 10-year-old boy, *"What am I gonna say?"* I assured him that I was just going to ask him some questions, to which he responded with a smile, *"I think I'll just say maybe to everything."* Now, a lot of parents would have seen that as their child being difficult or combative, but in that moment, I knew, Kai was once again showing me a truth that was of value to children and adults alike.

How many times in our lives have we said maybe, or I don't know, when in reality, we do know the answer, but are afraid of that small chance we might be wrong. Or that answering correctly will say something about who we are, that we'll be seen as a showoff or a know it all. So, we take the easy route and say, maybe.

Kai's been playing baseball for years, but for a while there every time we got in the car to drive to practice, he would start getting really upset, to the point where there were alligator tears and neither his dad nor I could figure out what was going on. Finally, one afternoon, I realized the reason Kai was getting so upset was because he was afraid. I let him know that it's okay to be scared, grownups get scared too, all the time. That's a part of life that never goes away. The difference now, is that I know if I'm not at least a little scared about something, it probably means I don't care. So, when I do get start experiencing feelings of fear around something, I also get excited, because I know it's something big that I really care about.

We sat down and I asked Kai what it was that was scaring him. He told me, through tears, that he was afraid of getting hit by the ball, because it hurts! What can I say, my kid is honest. I agreed with him. It definitely hurts to get pegged by the ball, just like it can hurt when we fail at something. But the quicker we learn that life is always going to be filled with little failures and start to see those failures as opportunities to learn something, the sooner we're able to stop getting hurt, and move onto the next exciting adventure. Sometimes life requires that we do the scary things, to prove to ourselves that we won't die.

I'm curious new friend, how many times has something scared you, and out of fear of the unknown, you talked yourself out of even trying? Or, self-sabotaged your way out of the situation because you were too scared that you might be laughed at, get hurt, or be seen as a failure, even if only in your own mind. The only people that truly fail are the ones who never show up.

I went on to ask Kai how he liked to be coached while playing sports. Does he like having a coach that yells, or someone that speaks kindly, explaining things clearly and taking time to answer questions? I asked him, how does he talk to himself, when he thinks about what he's doing, the new things he's trying, and the mistakes he's made. It's important that we remember to talk to and think about ourselves in the same way we want others to treat us — the same way in which we talk to others. While Kai agreed, this was also about the time he decided he was more interested in playing his video game than answering any more of my questions.

Throughout my career, in working with hundreds of individuals, in countless situations, I've found that no matter how confident, technically proficient, or financially well off someone is, we all share the common trait of allowing fear to hold us back from doing or having the things we want in life. This is more prevalent for some than others, but too often instead of admitting that the reason we're holding back is fear, we make excuses. *'I don't have time.' 'It's too expensive.' 'I don't know how.'* Instead of answering honestly, *'I'm scared shitless, and I really want this in my life, but I literally have no clue how to get there on my own.'* However, it's when these people, you and I, have a voice inside of us that gets so loud, it can't be squished down anymore, that we start to push through that fear and show up for ourselves. Taking even the tiniest of steps, moving towards the things that we want.

Becoming a parent and experiencing all this again, through my son's eyes, watching as he works through challenges, faces his fears, and comes out the other side has been amazing. I'm grateful every day that I've invested so much in my own personal development because now, I have the words, the experiences, to model for Kai how to handle things in healthier ways than I did, that it's okay to be scared, it's okay to try things that you don't know how to do, and it's okay to admit that you need help. As stubborn adults, we can often be too prideful to admit that we might need help, or don't know where to look, to find the support of someone who can help.

This is one of the big reasons I launched the podcast, why I'm writing this book, and why I launched the Beauty Insiders Membership. Having the right people in your network, people that are ready and willing to answer questions, explore possibilities, and celebrate the power of community over competition. Because none of us are meant to do this thing alone — life or business.

One practice that's had a huge hand in allowing me to work through my own fears, and develop a better trust in my intuition, is breathwork. Not only has it helped me to release a lot of the expectations I had for myself and how my life should be, but it's helped me to work through emotions and experiences in my past, that I didn't realize were weighing me down. I've enrolled in trainings to learn more about how breathwork affects the body, as well as the many benefits associated with regular practice. You may laugh but I actually tape both my boyfriend and my mouths shut at night while we sleep, so we're able to breath only through our noses. Because you're so caught up in the rhythm of your breaths, you're unable to think about much of anything else.

A good friend of mine, Corey Phelps, a Master NLP Practitioner, Clinical Hypnotherapist, and Business & Life Success Coach started her own breathwork journey through yoga, connecting her breath with movement and describes breathwork as being a powerful practice that fill you with feelings of being centered, in flow, and on fire with brilliant ideas.

Breathwork has also allowed me to experience more of my feminine energy. For the first 15 years of my career, I was operating from a very masculine place, making decisions based on logical thinking, not really listening to my heart or intuition. When faced with a choice I would ask myself, *What's going to get me to the next step? What's going to make me more money? What's going to advance my career?* Then, when I had my son, my perspective shifted, and I started looking at things more from how I felt. I started moving my trust from my head, into body and allowing myself to really feel into what it was that I needed. I started asking myself new questions, Do I need to move my body? Do I need to spend time getting stuff out through therapy, journaling, or physical movement? Were the foods I was eating making me feel a certain way? At first, the way I felt while meditating or practicing breathwork freaked me the fuck out, it was that powerful. But, now through regular practice, I've reawakened my natural intuition, and feel confident in trusting the wisdom that comes from within myself.

As entrepreneurs it can be difficult, to trust that little voice inside. We can get so caught up in the busyness of serving client after client, especially within the beauty industry, and find ourselves existing solely in our heads, versus trusting our gut. But I urge you, give it a try. It wasn't until I discovered breathwork that I was able to tap back into my body, face my fears, and make the changes necessary to pivot my business. To allow myself to be new at something, to fail, and learn the lessons I needed to grow.

Jessica Burgio

Listen to your inner voice when she's speaking softly like a *whisper* don't wait until she's *screaming!*

-Kiki Shiple

7 Questions to Ask Yourself NOW

After spending 20 years as a beauty professional, I've finally made the decision to leave the familiar space of hairdressing and explore the amazing adventures life has in store for me next. As I've been reflecting on the time I've spent behind the chair, one big realization that keeps coming up for me is that I haven't ever really given myself credit for all the shit I've accomplished. Until now.

I've included here a handful of questions, 7 to be exact, that I've been using to reflect personally, and encourage you to ask yourself. Pull out a pen & notebook, or a stack of post-its that you can stick to this page and revisit later. Give yourself a few moments to really think about each question, and journal on whatever thoughts come up for you.

Question 1: Am I playing small?

For me, playing small often looks like not showing up as my unapologetic self on social media. I say that I want to grow my brand, my business, that I want to be a thought leader, but then don't show up, because I get stuck in my ego of perfectionism. Maybe I'm not feeling like I look my best, or I record something and don't feel like it came out quite right. I know at my core that I'm overthinking things and keeping myself from growing. I'm playing small. Finally deciding to start the podcast and share my message with the world has definitely played in big part in helping me grow out of that crippling perfectionism, and step more steadily into a leadership role, but there are still ways that I can improve.

How might you be playing small in your life? Perhaps you're blocking yourself from accomplishing the things you want by telling yourself that you don't deserve them? Maybe you're not allowing yourself to try new things because you're afraid of showing up authentically? Maybe you're playing small when it comes to your relationships? Is it in how you're showing up for your brand or business? Is it in how you choose to share (or not to share) your unique expertise and brilliance?

Once you've recognized how you're playing small in your life, start looking at some of the tiny steps you can take, to move to the next level. Is there a course you'd like to take? Is there a course you'd like to teach? Is there one thing you can commit to doing, every day, that will help you to stop playing small and move in the direction of your dream life?

_____

Question 2: How can I be bigger than this situation, problem, or issue? What do I need to do, to find strength in this situation, problem, or issue?

This one's a two-parter. When we find ourselves in the midst of an issue, facing certain struggles or problems in life, we get to ask ourselves, how can we be bigger than the problem in order to overcome it and see to the other side? The key here, is in getting through the situation at hand, and not becoming a part of the problem. At the end of the day, anything can be seen as a problem, it's up to us to choose. I talk with my clients about how powerful it can be to pause and shift their view from seeing things as huge insurmountable problems, to being nothing more than speed bumps along their path. Then asking themselves, _How is this situation or experience serving me in a greater way? How can I be bigger than this issue? How can I overcome it? How can I help in this situation? How can I walk away?_

Sometimes these 'speed bumps' with be situations where we need to find strength. Often, when we're pivoting, growing, or shifting, something unexpected happens and we have the choice to suffer, or to turn a tragic event into something good. Ask yourself, How can I find strength to work through, release, or accept the problem or situation that I'm in? How do I find strength? Can I lean on someone for support? Do I go inwards and sit with myself? Do I have boundaries or modalities that I used to cope with situations that challenge me?

Question 3: How can I celebrate this win?

Take a moment right now and think back to the things you've accomplished in the last year, the last quarter, the last month, the last week. Hell, what have you accomplished so far today? Too often we only celebrate the BIG wins we have, like taking first place in a competition, landing a HUGE client, buying a new house, NOT punching a Karen. But when was the last time you recognized the smaller wins that you've achieved? So many of my clients tell me that they don't celebrate the little things, because they're just that, little. But I've got news for you, we don't achieve BIG wins without first accomplishing the little ones.

So, take the time, and make a list of the things you're proud of having accomplished. Maybe you've raised your prices, made an investment in yourself, taken a vacation, bought yourself a new bag, saved a certain amount of money, paid off a credit card. Some of my favorite moments are celebrating those seemingly small wins with my clients, friends, and colleagues. If you have something you want to celebrate and would like a little extra love, post your win, and tag me on IG. Ask yourself, How can I celebrate this win?

Question 4: How can I learn from this failure?

After we celebrate our wins, it's also important to acknowledge when shit didn't go right. I've been there. When I first started out doing hair, nobody wanted a cut from the new girl. Then, when I started coaching, my DMs went unanswered, and no-one wanted to invest in my services. But instead of getting frustrated, getting angry, and giving up, I asked myself, what can I learn from these failures? This question is a powerful one because the answers we find help to create a roadmap of what has worked.

Now, I'm a huge proponent of the premise that we don't fail, we learn, we grow, and we try again. But, throughout that trial-and-error process, we get to ask ourselves, What can I learn from this experience? Maybe you lost a job. Maybe you lost a client. Maybe you didn't get that promotion you were vying for, and it felt like a failure. Maybe you tried something, and it didn't work out quite like you'd hoped. Maybe you launched something new, a new product or service, and you were met with crickets. Ask yourself, How can I learn from this failure?

Question 5: Where am I not listening to myself?

This question is a biggie because it starts to bring up the idea of boundaries, and how we can better listen to the intuitive gift we all have with us, that so many of us ignore. We already know the answer to so many more things than we give ourselves credit for. One of my good friends, Kiki Shiple, once told me, "Listen to your inner voice when she's speaking softly like a whisper, don't wait until she's screaming." Prioritize yourself, your wellbeing, checking in on your boundaries and doing the things that support your mental, physical, emotional, and spiritual well-being. So, where are you not listening to yourself?

Question 6: Am I tolerating anything that isn't serving me?

As a perfectionist people pleaser, I tolerate a lot of shit that's not serving me. I've gotten better, but there are still many times where I say yes to things when I know I should be saying no. Other people's visions, ideas, beliefs, and causes that don't align with my own desires, my own path, or what I'm seeking to create. In 2021, my work for the year was 'peace' and I made a conscious effort to let go of anything and everything that didn't bring me peace. It wasn't easy, leaving relationships, backing away from friends, and opting out of business opportunities, but at the end of the day, I know the decisions I made were for the best. Because I was choosing to stop tolerating the things that were no longer serving me.

Sounds simple, but I think we all know, easier said than done. The best way to start is by checking in with yourself, asking, Am I tolerating anything that isn't serving me? Maybe you'll realize that you're tolerating going out and having a few drinks every weekend, but then feel like shit the rest of the week. Or you find that you're tolerating allowing clients to manipulate you into working longer hours than you need or want to. By uncovering that which is no longer serving you, you'll be able to begin the process of redefining your boundaries and saying so long to the things you're finished with. Ask yourself, Am I tolerating anything that isn't serving me?

Question 7: Where am I doing things that might be blocking my energy?

If you're overspending energy on certain things in life, it can wind up blocking or stifling the energy you need to create or do other things. I'll give you an example, one that my hairdressing clients aren't happy about. For the longest time, I was tolerating making the money I did behind the chair because it was good money, but that was no longer a situation or experience that served me. And being behind the chair was blocking the energy I needed, to create the next big thing in my life. Hint: The podcast, this book, and the Beauty Insiders Membership are all a part of that BIG thing!

I still appreciate and understand that everything I've done in the past, owning a salon, selling the salon, working behind the chair for 20 years, these are all parts of my journey, but they no longer served who I am now. So, being able to step away from my career as a beauty professional, being able to take the energy I was using to serve my clients from behind the chair, I'm now able to focus that energy on creating epic content for the podcast, writing this book, having insightful conversations with other badass accidental entrepreneurs, and working with clients 1:1 to support them in creating their own dream life, however that might look for them. Ask yourself, Where am I doing things that might be blocking my energy?

Jessica Burgio

People with half your talent are achieving twice as much. Because they're out there doing it, while you're still *waiting to feel ready*

Starting Scared

There's a really great quote that seems to pop up at least once a month on my IG or Pinterest feed, and I'm sure it's not just me, you've probably seen it too.

People with half your talent are achieving twice as much. Because they're out there doing it, while you're still waiting to feel ready.

Mic Drop! Seriously though! You're the secret sauce honnay! Whether you're already a successful small business owner with dreams of scaling, an entrepreneurial hopeful scared shitless of making the wrong move, or a side-hustling freelancer waiting for a sign, just do it! Scale, make a move, take the leap - Here's your sign!

Start scared! That's another hot-button phrase that's being thrown around like confetti at a 5-year old's birthday party - start scared.

As often as we hear it, 'start scared' is another one of those great quips that go in one ear & out the other. Those grand ideas that we love to think we'll follow through on, someday. We save them to our latest Inspirational Pinterest Board. Maybe even print them out & stick them on the fridge with a snarky magnet. If you're really committed, you get it tattooed somewhere badass, like the side of your finger, or in place of your eyebrow.

And, while each of these are definitely actions, some more permanent than others, they're also distractions, keeping you from doing the one thing you really want to do.

The business you want to launch.

The brand you want to build.

The course you want to create.

The product you want to develop.

The movement you want to start.

The change you want to make in the world.

Sure, we see the quote - start scared - and we understand that it's a great idea, but it never really sinks in enough to make us take BIG action. Until now. The idea of starting scared is something that comes up all the time when I'm coaching my clients and networking with other creative professionals, and usually includes an onslaught of buts!

But what if someone else is already doing it?

But what if it takes forever?

But what if I change my mind?

But what if I fail?

The fear of failure can be debilitating, even more so for us accidental entrepreneurs - because when we do something, it isn't just our head that's getting involved, it's our heart too. Starting scared means being aware of that fear and doing it anyway. I'm pretty sure that's another hot button quote.

It's normal to be afraid of failure, in fact, if we're being perfectly honest, I'm willing to bet that you've failed in the past, I know I have, and you're going to fail again. But, unless your big new idea involves swimming with hungry sharks or bungee jumping without the bungee, then the chance of you dying while going after what you want is pretty slim. Of course, I'm not technically a doctor, so I can't give you a fancy medical guarantee, but when was the last time you heard of someone dying because they started a business, or launched a new brand?

For curiosity's sake, when was the last time you heard of someone who went on to live happily ever after, feeling fulfilled, empowered, and like an MF'ing badass because they'd done the damned thing and followed their dreams? I can think of 10 people off the top of my head that will gladly show you their receipts.

But I digress. There are hundreds, thousands even, of entrepreneurs who are BIG names in the world, seen as the Oprah of their industries, but who flopped at least a few times before they made it big. Did you know that Vera Wang wasn't born as a badass high-end fashion designer? In fact, it wasn't until after she'd failed to make it onto the US Figure Skating team and was turned down for the Editor in Chief position with Vogue that she decided to pursue designing wedding dresses.

How about Arianna Huffington, co-founder of The Huffington Post. She's now the extremely well-known author of 15 different books, but before launching The Huffington Post, her second book was rejected by 36 different publishers!

Alright, one more, Evan Williams. Before co-founding Twitter, Evan developed a podcasting platform called Odeo, which flopped when Apple added podcasts to their iTunes platform at about the same time.

All three of these phenomenal individuals have gone on to do some pretty amazing things in their respective fields, but none of them were overnight successes who hit it out of the ballpark on their first try. Nope, they started scared - and when they experienced failure, in some pretty big ways, they dusted themselves off and tried again. Bonus points if you now have Miss Aaliyah stuck in your head. You're welcome.

The point I'm trying to make is that if you keep waiting until you're ready, the stars are aligned, the money's in the bank, you know everything, and you have zero worries about taking that next step, you'll be waiting forever. Now I'm in no way suggesting that you go out and apply for a million-dollar line of credit, hire a team of 20, and start writing your acceptance speech for Top New Business of The Year - but I do recommend that you start taking a serious look at what steps you can take today, tomorrow, next week - to make your dreams a reality.

The first step is to get a clear idea of what it is you're actually wanting to do. Are you looking at starting a new business, scaling a business you already have, developing a partnership with someone, or rebranding your existing business? Maybe you're wanting to shift your focus from one niche to another, or completely revamp the products or services you're offering. Take some time, find a quiet space where you can sit down and write this out. Whether you prefer to use a pen and paper, your laptop, or record things in a voice memo on your phone, what matters most is that you're being completely honest with yourself about what it is you're wanting to do.

Getting all of your thoughts, ideas, wants, desires, crazy schemes, and grand plans out of your head so you can take a look at them - deciding what's possible, what's plausible, and what might be a little bit of a bigger stretch. Once you've got everything written down, read through what you have. Make sure that nothing is missing and that everything you've jotted down describes in detail what it is that you're wanting. If possible, trim those notes down to a few lines that capture what you're setting out to do. This can become your intention, your goal.

Next, you'll want to make sure you know who it is you'll be serving. Is your desired audience the same as you've been working with previously or is that going to change as well. It's extremely important that we know who it is we want to be working with so that when we make this big leap, we have a clear idea of who we're talking to. I'm sure we've all heard the quote by Seth Godin, "*When you speak to everyone, you speak to no one.*" Look at how far you are already. You know exactly what it is that you want, what you're going to be focusing on, what your intention is, and who you're communicating with.

Take a deep breath — like really deep. Are you feeling a little less scared yet? Even the tiniest bit more prepared to pursue what you want, sticking your tongue out at your fear and starting anyway? Knowing what you want, and who you want to work with is a great start. My good friend and fellow podcast host, Angie Lee, recently coined the phrase "start before you're ready."

The next thing you'll want to do is ask yourself, what is it that I can bring to this industry, to this audience? What is it about you that makes the business, brand, service, or product you're going to create different from the other options already available? What makes you stand out from the competition? What skills, knowledge, experience, expertise, certifications, education, background do you have that others might not? What receipts do you have to show?

Compiling all of this should not only help boost your confidence in this amazing new venture but will also serve to show your audience that you know what's up! We so often forget that not everyone has the same badass skills & expertise as we do. We take for granted that we're one in a million - and no matter what it is we set out to do in life, we're doing it with our own flair and magic. You're a pretty big deal and it's about time you started believing it!

I'm not going to lie and tell you that you'll never experience imposter syndrome ever again. Hell, I've been doing this for years, and KNOW that I'm a badass, and I still have bouts of imposter syndrome sneak up on me every so often. Usually, it's when I'm contemplating making a big investment in myself, or my business. But I've learned over time, and with practice, that if I let that nagging voice stop me from doing what I really want, pursuing my dreams, and living the life I've always imagined, I regret it.

Without fail.

Every. Single. Time.

We're all human. We all have doubts, hesitations, worries, and fears. But, if you wait until you're 100% ready, and no longer scared of the million little things that might happen, you'll miss out on experiencing what does happen.

When you take the leap.

Launch the business.

Create the course.

Develop the product.

Start the movement.

Change the world.

I encourage you, to ask yourself, what's on your heart, what is it that you really, really want. Imagine how your life might change were you to be where you want to be, right now. Allow yourself to get excited about the prospect of new adventures, experiences, successes, and lessons learned. Remember, the greats weren't born that way. They learned to walk, talk, spell, and drive just like the rest of us. But, when faced with the choice between staying comfortable & safe or exploring new, sometimes scary, possibilities - they opted to leap! They trusted themselves enough to start scared.

So, what're you waiting for? What do you really want? And what's the first step you can take towards making that dream a reality?

Jessica Burgio

Take action.

Even if it's weird, sticky, messy action.

Just do it!

Find Your Tribe

I firmly believe in the power of connection, getting in the right rooms, and the power of community — that's where the magic happens. This is one of the driving forces behind my podcast, being able to sit down with so many amazingly powerful individuals, hearing their stories, where they started, what they've struggled with, and what they've accomplished — then being able to share that with my audience, my worldwide community. I felt like I'd found my tribe, my people, that first day I stepped into the Robert Cromeans salon as a newly graduated hairdresser, and I feel that same spark every time I connect with a fellow creative, accidental entrepreneur, making their mark on the world in whatever way feels right to them.

So many of my podcast guests, clients, and colleagues have a similar story of meeting one person that completely changed the trajectory of their life. Maybe it was a mentor, someone they looked up to, or someone who showed them what could be possible if they stopped allowing fear to block their potential. The key, as so many really smart and successful folks will tell you, is to surround yourself with people who inspire you to be better, to challenge yourself, and to question assumptions.

When I was first getting started, shifting my business from full time hairdressing to exploring what it might look like, to be a coach for other beauty professionals, I knew that I was going to need to make investments, in myself and my new business. Dropping large chunks of cash on something that isn't a physical or material product, something you can't touch, taste, or smell, but instead something that you feel in your gut, in your confidence, in your heart. But, like I tell my clients, sometimes you have to pay to get into the room when you're first starting out.

For me, making the investment to be a part of the Fast Foundation's Mastermind group was something I would do again in a heartbeat. Yes, the investment was big and scary, and the results were unknown, but I knew that I needed to be in that room. Connecting with those people, learning what they knew, and soaking in as much of their genius as I possibly could. Walking into that room on the first day, I didn't know what I didn't know, but I was willing to take the chance, on myself, and on these powerful individuals who had built lives, businesses, brands, communities, movements that inspired me.

Now, a quick note on mentors. A lot of people believe that to be a mentor you need to know it ALL. But I challenge that assumption. I believe that to be a successful mentor you need only be at least one step ahead of the people you're supporting. Everything in life is changing, constantly. Whether it be a new algorithm online, a new twist on marketing, the best course delivery software, or networking via AI instead of in person. To expect anyone to know everything is setting all parties involved up for disappointment. So, be proud of where you are, and what you know. We each have our own areas of expertise that can be shared with others, whether as a paid mentor, or energetically exchanged with someone who possesses an expertise different than your own.

As the amazing Marie Forleo so eloquently says, *'Everything is Figureoutable.'* But why spend 400 hours on Google and YouTube trying to figure something out when you could reach out to someone within your community, your tribe, that can lend you their expertise, saving you time and headaches.

For at least 10 years, I dreaded going to networking groups or events. They were something that definitely left me feeling like something was missing. Have you ever attended a party or gathering where you didn't recognize anyone and had a moment of panic, wondering if you were in the wrong place? That's exactly how networking groups made me feel. The room always seemed to be filled with stuffy people who were in corporate positions, shooting the shit, and comparing cubicle war stories. Oh, and we can't forget the old school mentality of only allowing a single person from each industry into the group, because, who wants to deal with variety, right?

Sure, those networking groups worked for some people, and probably worked for some industries better than others. But I knew in my gut that they weren't the right place for me, or my people. There's something so powerful about looking around a room and being surrounded by people in the industry that you love, showing you what's possible if you keep doing your best.

While I owned my salon, I got to a point where I stopped going to any kind of networking events. I honestly thought that because I was making well over 6-figures, I knew what I was doing. I had a thriving career behind the chair, and I figured I didn't really have a need to explore what else was out there. I've got news for you though; we don't know what we don't know, and there's a big difference between having a routine, and being stuck in a rut. Keeping yourself open to being reinspired, and having a community, a tribe, filled with people who do just that, inspire you, is one of the most magical feelings in the world.

So, get out there, whether it be via social media, in your local community, or pulling out the good old phone book (do people actually have these anymore?), and start connecting with people you want in your tribe. Send emails, DM's, make phone calls, and connect with those creative badasses that inspire you to take action, even if it's weird, sticky, messy action. Your people are waiting!

How can you start connecting with your tribe?

How are you going to take action?

Jessica Burgio

Until the pain of not doing the things that you want or having what you want in your life is *greater than your excuses* you'll never grow beyond where you are now.

How Bad Do You Want It?

I like to keep it real and tell it like it is, whether I'm interacting with clients, colleagues, friends, or family. I'm not known for being soft spoken, blowing smoke, or beating around the bush. It's one of the traits that my clients say they love most about me — they know with absolute certainty that I'm going to call them out on their shit just as quickly as I'll be celebrating their achievements.

One of the big questions I ask when I first meet a fellow accidental entrepreneur or creative business owner is, *How bad do you want it?* You're probably thinking, *How bad do I want what?*

If you're anything like me, and if you're still reading this, I'm pretty sure you are, there was a point in your life when you had a dream. Maybe it was a side hustle, a seemingly crazy idea, or a goal that you wanted to achieve, something that could take you away from whatever business, job, or career you were already doing. Or maybe you're content with where you're at, you enjoy the work that fills your days, but are curious about if there might be something better, something different, out there.

At the end of the day, we have to ask ourselves, *How bad to I want it?* More often than not, when I present my clients or friends with this question, they don't actually answer but instead provide one of two excuses. ***I don't have the time and I don't have the money.***

Generally speaking, time and money are the two things that hold us back from doing the things we say we want to do, from accomplishing the things we say we want to accomplish. *I don't have time to work out. I don't have time to learn a new skill. I don't have the money to invest in that course or class. I don't, I don't, I don't.*

Personally speaking, I always had an excuse. I've never been someone with time to spare at any point in my life. I've always been a hustler who thrived being busy, but also knew that I wanted more, I needed more in my life. I got sick of my own excuses and decided to reverse engineer the process of getting where I wanted and doing it NOW.

When I was younger, I wanted to be an educator. I always wanted to teach in some way, and for the longest time I assumed that was a goal I had to give up. It wasn't until years later that I realized I had been teaching all along. While working as a professional hairdresser I mentored a ton of assistants, personally training a handful of amazingly talented stylists who've gone on to start successful salons of their own. Now, as a coach, brand strategist, and community leader, I teach on the daily. Whether it be 1:1 with my clients, in small groups at my new collaborative space in San Diego, through the podcast, the Beauty Insiders Membership, or now, through this book.

I challenge you to think about the way you spend your time. I know for me it helps to write it out. Now, I'm not saying you need to track every moment of every day, but I am saying that if you bring awareness to the ways you're spending time, you'll begin to notice the many opportunities you have, for making your dream life a reality.

Ask yourself: *How much time am I spending watching TV, every day, every week? How much time am I spending scrolling through social media? How much time am I spending watching hilarious videos of cats doing crazy shit?*

For many of us, we spend time with our families in the evenings, watching a movie or the latest reality show, and family time is important. But what if you took only one or two evenings a week, to spend that time on your side hustle, bringing your dream business to fruition?

Now, when it comes to money, you don't need to find an extra million dollars somewhere, although that would be nice. Think about some of the things that you're paying for every day, every week, every month, that you might be able to change up, to allocate funds towards pursuing your dreams. For me, this meant recognizing that I like good food, so when I got out to eat, I'm not going somewhere cheap. I still love going out for a nice dinner, but instead of doing this every other night, I treat myself once a week, making a point of having healthy groceries, or using a meal delivery service so I can eat well but for a much lower investment.

Another of my habits has been stopping to buy a coffee every afternoon. This was just something I did, and really didn't think about. Until I realized that I was dropping $8 on warm milk and espresso, every single day. That added up to $240/month, $2,920/year! I'm not saying cut out the coffee completely, but if you make a point of recognizing the areas where you can save a little time and money, and reallocate them to pursuing your dream business, career, or trip, the excuses disappear pretty quickly. Are there any small expenses that you could revisit to look at saving money to reallocate for your dream business?

Until the pain of not doing the things that you want or having what you want in your life is greater than your excuses, you'll never grow beyond where you are now.

Brace yourself for another dose of brutal honesty. It's up to you. All of it. Deciding to stop making excuses. Taking a hard look in the mirror and asking yourself: *How am I showing up for myself today, tomorrow, this week? What work am I doing that's going to move the needle in my business, my brand, my career, my life?* And, most of all, *How bad do I really want it?*

It's okay to want more in life. It's okay to dream bigger. Every morning, you get to start things anew and decide that no matter when kind of shit lands in your lap, you're finding the time, and the money, to do the things you want to do. To invest in the things, the experiences, you want. And, before you know it, you'll have the time, the money, and the life you've always wanted. I believe in you.

When it comes to being a successful accidental entrepreneur, it's all about

mindset, mindset, mindset

Mindset, Mindset, Mindset

You know how in Real Estate, they say the most important aspect of any home or property is location, location, location? Well, when it comes to being a successful accidental entrepreneur, it's all about mindset, mindset, mindset. Now, for any of you that are a little shy or unsure about exploring your woo side, let me tell you right now, don't be. It won't hurt a bit and you'll be shocked at how powerful it can be, to spend a little extra time paying attention to your own well-being.

Below, I'm sharing three beginner mindset hacks that have had serious impact on my own life, as well as the lives of my clients. I recommend making time to implement these three hacks at the beginning of your day, or before bed at night. You can also utilize these practices anytime you're experiencing any sort of overwhelm, burnout, depression, anxiety, or just feeling out of sorts.

Mindset Hack 1: Practice gratitude.

A gratitude practice can be as simple as opening your eyes in the morning and repeating in your head a few things that you're grateful for. Now, I'll be the first person to admit, if I've had a shitty day the day before, something didn't go right, I got in a car accident, or receiving a parking ticket, it can be hard to wake up and think positive, grateful thoughts first thing in the morning. It's so much easier and more natural for us to think or focus on the shit going on in our lives. And with that kind of thinking, it's no time at all before we're spiraling down the 'woe is me' slide, landing in 'my life sucks' bay. So, instead of letting life's shitstorm take hold, make a conscious effort of tapping into the basic things you're most grateful for. *I'm grateful for another day to move through this process. I'm grateful that the sun is shining, and I have time to make coffee this morning. I'm grateful that I get to see one of my good friends this afternoon.*

You may be surprised at how quickly you're able to progress from the more basic things (oxygen) and move onto the bigger pieces of your life that can so often be overlooked or taken for granted. Personally, I like to make a list of my gratitude's each morning, which is where mindset hack 2 comes in.

Mindset Hack 2: Journal regularly.

Journaling regularly doesn't have to look a certain way for everyone. Some folks prefer to journal with pen and paper, others use their cell phone, and yet others record voice memos to themselves to capture their thoughts. A great way to start is by keeping a small journal or notebook by your bed and jotting down a list of the things your grateful for every morning. Not only does this help solidify the items within your daily gratitude practice, but it also helps to develop a regular writing or journaling routine.

Next, it's important that we do what's often called a free write. This simply means allowing our brains to dump out everything that happened the day before, week before, months before, and getting it onto paper. Spelling doesn't matter, grammar doesn't matter, heck, your journaling doesn't even have to be legible. No one else ever needs to be able to read it, in fact sometimes it's better that way. What matters is that you begin a regular practice of writing out whatever it is you're feeling.

Some mornings your entry is going to be really long, some days it's going to be short and sweet, but as with any other habit or routine, it's important that you give yourself that window of time, 10-15 minutes, to free write and let whatever's coming up for you, come out. It's an amazing feeling, being able to leave the worries, thoughts, and frustrations from the day before in that book beside your bed and moving on to tackle the day ahead.

Many of my clients like to have a second journal as well, someplace they can use to write their goals, intentions, and dreams they intend to manifest. These can be fun, especially when you're journaling these achievements as if they've already come to fruition.

For example, if you're interested in having more public speaking opportunities on large stages, you may journal, *I'm proud of myself for having the confidence to show up to speak so powerfully on the TEDx stage earlier this year.* You may never have been invited to speak on a stage of that size yet, but your future self wants to speak there, and they want to do it confidently.

Mindset Hack 3: Move your body.

A few years ago, when my mom had cancer, I found myself dealing with a lot of stuck energy and a lot of uncomfortable feelings. I experienced guilt and shame around not spending enough time with her, as well as feelings of overwhelm, exhaustion, and burnout. I knew I needed to find a healthy way to process what I was experiencing.

I've always been a really active person and during this time when I was processing so many unfamiliar thoughts and feelings, I stopped listening to music, and would instead go on what I started calling clarity runs or walks. At the time, I was living at the beach, and would push myself, my body, and my emotions, to the point where I was able to release everything I was feeling, through sweat, laughter, and tears. Moving my body helped me to not only reminisce on memories I hadn't thought of in years, but also to process the thoughts and feelings I was being overwhelmed with.

To this day I still go on clarity runs or walks, and now see most of my workouts differently. Instead of viewing them as simply physical workouts for my body, I see them as my own personal moving meditations. I know that when I have a lot on my mind, and need to process big things, I need to be moving, to release that energy, but I also want to focus on my positive mantras and affirmations. Instead of worrying about if I'm 'doing it wrong' I ask myself, what does my body need from me today? Sometimes, it needs to get hyped up, meaning I turn up the gangster rap and ride the Peloton bike. Or maybe I need a slower paced workout, a quiet walk on the beach listening to the water and sea birds while repeating a positive mantra to myself.

Now, you may not be a runner, and you don't have to be. Maybe for you, movement is a brisk walk outside, a bike ride, practicing yoga, or any other modality that allows you to connect and really feel your body and emotions.

What's great about these three hacks is that they can be done together or separately, depending on your schedule, and what you feel you need the most. I like to allow myself extra time on days where I know I have a lot of big things going on, so I can really set myself up for success by having my mindset on point. And, while these three mindset hacks can serve as powerful tools to start a ripple within your life, it's also important that you give yourself permission to honor where you're at. So often we find ourselves always looking to the future, and all of the behaviors we want to change or improve, that we forget to appreciate who and where we are now, today, and all of the hard work we've already done, to get this far.

Jessica Burgio

It's important to ask yourself, is this really a *good opportunity* or is it a distraction in disguise?

Indecisive No More

Let's talk indecisiveness. Huge word, right? But how often do we actually stop to think about what it means?

We've all been in situations where we *should* ourselves into a corner. *Should* I do this. *Should* I do that. Maybe yes. Maybe no. I don't know about you but for me, living in that place of indecision feels icky, chaotic, and like the world is spinning out of control. It also makes me feel like I frantically need to make a decision, ANY decision, right away. Which doesn't often wind up with the best results.

Sometimes the decisions that give us the greatest pause are the smallest ones. How many fights have you gotten into with your significant other over where to have dinner? *Where do you want to eat? I don't know, where do you want to eat? I don't know. Do you want steak or burgers? Do you want to stay in or go out?* Of course, this is indecision on a super small scale, but look at how powerful it can be. These seemingly inconsequential moments of indecisiveness can often make or break a relationship, leaving you feeling resentful, frustrated, or unfulfilled by the decisions that have to be made for you, instead of by you.

So, I'm curious, how are you showing up on a day-to-day basis? Do you see yourself as being someone who knows exactly what they want, at all times, never hesitating or seeking the recommendations of others? Are you someone who likes to take a poll of the room before making any decisions yourself. Or do you prefer to wait on the sidelines until someone else makes those decisions for you?

One of my favorite things to talk about with my clients, colleagues, and friends, are non-negotiables. Our non-negotiables are the decisions we've made in advance when we're in an emotionally sound and balanced place. For example, a non-negotiable may be that you always put $200/week into a savings or emergency fund. No matter how much you've made each week, how tight the budget is, or if you're relaxing on a white sandy beach. Every week, you sign into your bank account and transfer $200 into that account.

Often in life, we're called on to make big decisions when we're not in an emotionally sound place. This can look like saying yes to things you'd really rather say no to. It can look allowing your boundaries to be railroaded over because you want to please others. This can also look like making rash decisions because of an insinuated threat of scarcity. Luckily, when we take the time NOW to become clear on our individual non-negotiables, it's much easier to ignore these distractions and stay the course, continuing to move in the direction of what we really want, how we desire to show up in our life, in business, and what feels right for us.

For a long time, I struggled with SOS, Shiny Object Syndrome, or as some people call it, Squirrel Brain. I'm super creative and love to fly by the seat of my pants. As much as I love and crave structure, I also thrive with absolutely no structure at all. So, there've been numerous times in the past, where I've lived in that place of indecisiveness. But there comes a point where our brains start to really get uncomfortable with being indecisive. When I'm able to dig in my heels and really commit to the why behind what I'm doing, I no longer have to wonder if I'm making the right choice.

It's important to ask yourself, is this really a good opportunity, or is it a distraction in disguise?

I have a cousin who can barely walk, and while I've always been an active person there are still days where I don't feel like working out. On those days, I think about her, I think about how I have this amazing opportunity to explore what my body can do. I think about how fortunate I am to still be here, in the shape I am, doing what I love most in the world, while there are so many people who don't have the luxury of making their own choices. When I'm on an especially hard run, or in the middle of a project that seems daunting, when I really want nothing more than to quit whatever it is I'm doing, I think about the opportunities I have, and why I've made the decisions I have. While the run still may suck, and the project may leave me pulling out my hair, I still know that I'm better for the decisions I've made.

When we're able to start making decisions that are in the interest of the best version of our higher self, crushing the goals we set for ourselves isn't a matter of *if*, but *when*. I know what level I want to play at, and for me to show up in that way, I have to be crystal clear, fiercely protective, and decisive on what and who I allow to utilize my energy and share my space.

So, you may be thinking. *Sounds great Jess, but how do I move from wobbly squirrel brain to decisive and determined?* Well, I'm glad you asked!

If someone in your life, this may be a friend, family member, partner, colleague, or client, starts treating you in a way that doesn't feel right, you have two choices. You speak up, say something about it, and explore having a conversation with them about how you'd prefer to be treated. In that moment, it's not a decision, it's a discussion. And having open ended, respectful discussions where you're able to share your position, is standing up for the best interested of your higher self and the first step to setting healthy boundaries. It's at that point where you're able to make the decision for yourself, if this person is able and willing to treat you in the way you require, great, if not, then you get to close that door.

If you're someone who struggles with indecision frequently, start small. Maybe you have a goal of getting more sleep at night, and not drinking alcohol during the week. But a group of friends invite you out for happy hour on a Thursday evening. You can still go out with your friends, if that's what you want to do, but let them know you'll be heading home early, and sipping on iced tea, hold the Long Island. Being decisive about what you want, and what best serves your higher self doesn't mean saying no to having fun or being spontaneous. It simply means putting your interests, your goals, your dreams, your desires, at the top of your personal priority list.

Some people call these commitments sacrifices. And at times, it may feel that way. But, if we make decisions based on what feels good right now, we'll say yes to everything. Trust me, I've done the research personally. How many times have you committed at 9am, to going out with friends for drinks later that evening? And then by 7:30, when you're supposed to be getting ready, you're really wishing you'd said no. Then, because you don't want to be seen as a flake, you pull on your big girl panties, go out with the girls, and have an okay time, but get home so late that you're tired the next day, a little hungover, and feeling like a bloated mess because of all the greasy food and sugary drinks. Now, you're feeling guilty, because you'd told yourself you weren't going to eat French fries or drink during the week, and because you're feeling guilty for letting yourself down, you spend the day not only feeling like shit, but mentally beating yourself up over the choices you made.

That guilt, shame, and icky shitty feeling is basically a residual effect of not staying in your power, of not sticking to your own non-negotiables, and not having healthy boundaries in place.

When I was participating in bodybuilding competitions back in the day, one of the biggest challenges I faced came when I would set massive goals for myself, to see how far I could push myself, how fit I could get, and how well I could place. But, because this also meant setting strict non-negotiables for myself, like not drinking, not eating sweets or greasy foods, getting plenty of sleep, waking up super early to be at the gym, it also meant saying no to a lot of friends. After three or four months of saying no to people, they stop asking you to hang out. That was tough, but I also knew that I had a goal, a vision, and they had their own. It wasn't my place to judge theirs, just as it wasn't their place to judge mine. But, like everything in life, our goals, visions, and non-negotiables will change as we do.

One night I did go out with the girls to celebrate a friend's birthdays. Everyone else was drinking, but I was still training so I ordered something low calorie or no calorie, and non-alcoholic. I remember thinking that I looked really good, I felt really good about how well I was doing, but I wasn't actually enjoying myself, being out with friends who were all drinking, while I sat sober in the corner. I'll be honest – I was frustrated, angry, and edging on blaming them for making me feel a certain way. But then, something clicked inside of me, and I realized, I decide how I feel, and I decide what my non-negotiables are, my goals, my visions, my dreams. I remember being overwhelmed with gratitude and excitement, knowing that I was living my best life, and my friends were amazing for having invited me. They were also super lucky to have a responsible friend to drive their drunk ass's home. Oh, and I knew that I was going to feel like a million bucks at the gym in the morning, while they were all hungover and hiding from the sun.

When we're able to shift our perspective and remember that the non-negotiables we're setting for ourselves are for the greater good, for our own betterment, and that it's okay if other people don't understand. Strive to make your decisions from a place of being emotionally sound, not in the heat of the moment, based on who you want to be, and the highest most spectacular version of yourself.

Ask yourself, what are some of your personal non-negotiables?

Jessica Burgio

For too long, I stayed in a box, bit my tongue, and told myself that I wasn't smart enough, I sold myself & my expertise short.

No More!

Let Your Voice Be Heard

One of the most downloaded podcast episodes I've recorded so far was when I pulled back the curtain about what it looks like to start a podcast. Now, I want to start this chapter with a caveat that the information I'm providing is what I'm learned and experienced through my own podcasting journey. There are definitely going to be other opinions, and options available, but this book is my opportunity to share with you, my new friend, what's worked for me, in hopes of giving you a leg up in the game.

Podcasting has been an amazing way to explore the topics that I enjoy talking about most. It's allowed me a platform to meet new people, learn new things, and discover what turns me on, and what doesn't when it comes to my business and brand. So, if you're finding yourself curious about how podcasting can help broadcast your message to a worldwide audience, have a little fun, and possible even become an additional stream of income, read on.

I initially started the Beauty Inspires Beauty podcast as a way of giving back to the beauty industry and my fellow creative accidental entrepreneurs, by empowering them with information that I've learned over 20+ years in the industry, as well as inviting amazingly powerful and inspiring guests to share their stories, because really, knowledge is power, and community is key! I'm a huge fan of embracing the idea that I don't know what I don't know, and I'm super okay with that. What I'm not okay with is staying in the same place.

For too long, I stayed in a box and told myself that I wasn't smart enough, or advanced enough to have anything of real value to share with other beauty professionals. I kept my head down, and called myself 'just a hairdresser,' like it was an insult. I sold myself and my expertise short, telling myself that no one wanted to hear what I had to say, and my business didn't need to change or grow, because it was just a salon. I was just a hairdresser. What I was doing didn't matter in the grand scheme of things.

I was different then. The industry was different then. 21 years ago, we all used paper calendars and notepads to book our appointments. If you were lucky, you had a front desk service helping field phone calls and schedule your clients, but for most of us, that was just a part of our daily job. The beauty industry is leveling up more and more every year, and it seems like there's something new to learn every day. Even with the years of experience I had behind a chair, I still knew there was a shit ton of important stuff that I didn't know, and if I were to find a way to connect with people who DID know what I didn't, and were willing to share that wisdom with myself and my audience, it could change the lives of more accidental entrepreneurs than I could ever hope to on my own.

Basically, I got sick of my own shit, turned my dream of having a podcast into a reality, and now, 100+ episodes later, I've been offered a position co-hosting another podcast, this one associated with the Fast Foundation's Mastermind group that helped me get started in the first place!

Podcasting is a great platform to explore if you enjoy chatting with other people or can speak on a topic for more than a few minutes. If you like shorter snippets, I recommend sticking to TikTok or IG, but if you want to really dig into a question, an assumption, a hot topic, or interview, podcasting could be a great fit for you. Another thing that's great about podcasts, is that only you've recorded each episode, you can then chunk it out into bite sized pieces of other content, like social media posts, email campaigns, and blog posts.

Included below are seven key tips to help you successfully start a podcast for your business or brand. I've also created a free download of these eight points that you can snag on my website (www.bit.ly/jesspodcastguide).

Tip 1: Ask yourself: Why am I starting a podcast?

It may seem obvious, but a lot of people skip this step, and wind up recording a single episode, then realize they don't know why they're doing it, and they stop. Ask yourself, What's my intention behind talking to an audience every week? Does a podcast serve my brand or mission?

What's the purpose behind my podcast? What kind of information do I want to share? What kind of guests do I want to have on?

_____

_____

_____

_____

_____

_____

_____

Tip 2: Ask yourself: What should I name my podcast?

This one depends on what you want to talk about and what the goal or intention is behind your new podcast. What's a catchy title that encompasses the topic, theme, or focus you're trying to connect with your audience on? Don't get too caught up on this. Come up with a couple ideas. Phone a friend. You can always change the title in the future if your audience or focus shifts.

_____

_____

_____

_____

_____

_____

_____

Tip 3: Ask yourself: Who is my podcast for?

Sit down and write out a paragraph explaining what your new podcast is going to be all about. If you're not totally clear on this, that's fine. Keep the paragraph broad and leave room for refinement. Make it simple and concise but provide enough information so your listeners know what the show's about. You can also use this paragraph as a recorded introduction to the podcast.

Tip 4: Create your new podcast logo & artwork on Canva

If you aren't familiar with Canva, I need you to put this book down and go register for a free account right now (www.canva.com). Canva has allowed small business owners with zero design experience to literally become graphic designers on a budget. Take a few minutes and look at the logos and cover artwork for some of your favorite podcasts, or other podcasts that are popular with your ideal audience. The accepted graphic size for iTunes is 1400x1400 pixels and can be used for any and all other platforms you choose to utilize. Below, jot down some notes about you like and don't like in logos or designs. What elements do you want to include? What colors do you like? What kind of fonts?

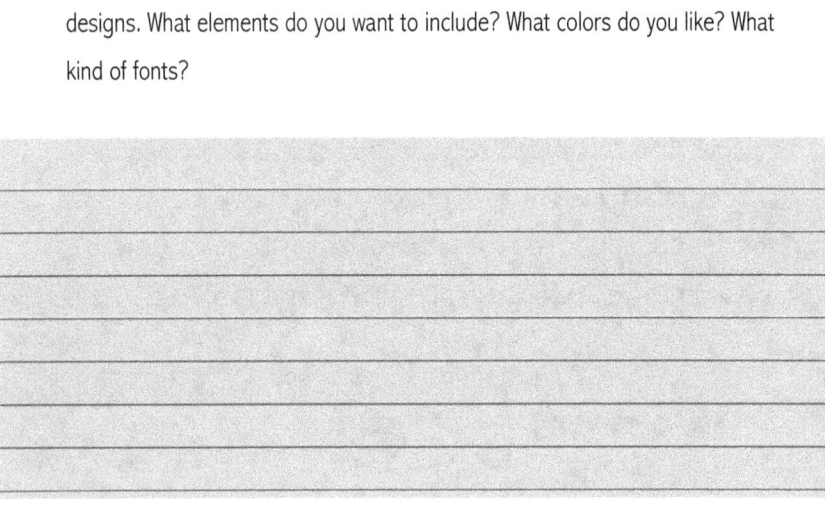

Tip 5: Make a list of the equipment or programs you need to get started

You can make this part as simple or as extravagant as you want. I ordered my original microphone setup from Amazon, and recently switched to using my son's gaming headphones that have a microphone attached. I record my episodes on Zoom and save them to Dropbox. If you're using a Mac, I know a lot of my fellow podcasters use GarageBand to edit their episodes, and there are plenty of websites where you can find and purchase royalty free music to use. Decide if you're wanting to make an investment into this area of your new podcast, or if you'd prefer to start with some of the free options.

Tip 6: Decide which platforms you want to post on

The answer is to this one, is ALL OF THEM. There are services available online that will blast your podcast episodes to every online platform available, or you can go through and add them manually. But you definitely want to take a few moments in the beginning to set things up for your podcast to be available to stream on every platform you can.

Tip 7: Plan a quick & dirty launch of your podcast on social media

I'm a community building & connection QUEEN. So, when I decided to launch a podcast, I decided to reach out to my community and ask them to help me with the launch, in hopes of reaching as many people as possible. I looked at my 6 most recent Instagram posts and made a list of all the people who were regularly liking or commenting on my photos. Then I thought about all my best friends, mentors, colleagues, and supporters. Next, I thought about all the people who have ever come to any event I've put together, whether it was a retreat, a webinar, a training, a happy hour, anything! Let me tell you, this gave me a seriously long list of people who already support and care about me, and I knew would want to be a part of the excitement around my new podcast launching.

I added them all to an email (BCC of course) and sent out a message asking if they'd like to be a part of my podcast launch, and to respond YES if they were. Once I'd received back a TON of emailed yes's, I created a slide in Canva (I told you, Canva is amazing), that included the artwork for the podcast as well as where it could be streamed. Then, I sent that slide out via email to the people who'd responded that they wanted to participate, over the course of 10 days. And just like that, I have 100+ people helping shout out my new podcast on their IG stories, to their audiences, for 10 days. It was amazing!

Remember, in life and business, you have to ask for what it is you want. And, when people answer YES to helping, make it as EASY as possible for them to do so. Provide them with the materials they need, remind them the night before, and thank them!

Make a list of your friends, mentors, colleagues and supporters that may want to help you announce your new podcast.

Jessica Burgio

I promise, taking action, even the tiniest, messiest action, will feel *so much better* than staying where you are now.

In Case of Emergency

'In case of emergency,' a phrase we see and hear all the time. *In case of emergency break the glass. In case of emergency push the big red button. In case of emergency run away in a zig zag pattern like your life depends on it.*

We've taken care to surround ourselves with all sorts of helpful escape hatches, for any number of different physically threatening or concerning situations. But, what about when the emergency is that we're feeling stuck, like Winnie the Pooh in that damned rabbit hole? What then?

This chapter is for those situations, those emergencies when you find yourself feeling stuck, whether in your current position, the business or brand you're creating, or even dreaming about what the future might hold. Consider this your own personal bitchslap, shocking you out of whatever rut you've tumbled into, and shining a light on a ladder you couldn't see before.

I've been where you are, slouching in defeat at the bottom of a pit, resigned to the fact that this is where I life now. Escape is impossible. Inconceivable. And I'm not talking just once. There've been times where I spent days, weeks, months in that hole. But I've also gotten really good at pulling myself back out.

So, to start, it's important to recognize that being stuck isn't always a bad thing, it can also be our higher selves giving us an opportunity to reassess the choices we have available, the situations we're in. Often, if we're feeling stuck, it can be directly related to a decision, conversation, or action steps that we know we need to take in order to move forward and create momentum, but for whatever reason, are scared or hesitant about.

When we lack clarity, we lack confidence.

I'd never equated the two together until I started to pivot in my own business and take on projects that required me to come off autopilot. We've all been paralyzed by indecision, inaction, or avoidance, I'm sure if you took a few moments right now, you'd be able to think of at least one conversation, text, or email that you've needed to tackle but have avoided for FAR too long, because it was uncomfortable. And sometimes, that conversation isn't with anyone else, it's with ourselves!

At the end of the day, we need to remember that success loves momentum. So, the longer we sit, festering in indecision, the longer it's going to take for us to find clarity and direction. How many times have you said that you wanted to wait to do something until you were ready? Well, brace yourself for another truth bomb, ready is a lie! Waiting to take action until you've lost the weight, learned the thing, are less busy, feel smarter, have more money, blah, blah, blah, until you feel 'ready' simply means that you're sitting, stuck, at the bottom of that pit, waiting for someone else to make a decision or choice for you.

Sure, it can be scary to make big decisions without first having ALL of the facts, but I promise, whatever worst-case scenario you have filling your head, stopping you from taking action and pursuing your dreams, the reality will never be that bad. I mean, unless your action is wrestling alligators, or jumping from a plane without a parachute. But let's be reasonable.

So, are you ready to break the glass, push the button, and take action to break out of being stuck? Included below are 5 questions I ask myself, anytime I'm feeling indecision creep in. They may not seem like much, but I can assure you, they've been game changers for myself as well as my clients. And often, it's the simplest thing, like taking a few moments to pause, check in with ourselves, and journal anything that's coming up, that can help make monumental changes in our lives.

Question 1: What decision, conversation or action am I avoiding?

Sometimes there's more than one situation or decision that comes to mind. Jot these down in a journal, notebook, or on your phone.

Question 2: If I take action on this situation or conversation, what's the absolute worst thing that could happen?

Seriously, what is the worst thing that could possibly happen to you? Is it that someone might be mad at you, have their feelings hurt, or perhaps they say 'no.'

Question 3: How would you handle that worst-case scenario?

Let's say shit hit the fan and your worst-case scenario did happen. What would you do next? How would you handle that?

Question 4: What's the best thing that could happen?

This is where we get to have a little fun. Think big. Sure, this may be improbable, but give yourself permission to dream here.

Question 5: How would you feel if the best-case scenario happened?

Visualize and embody how it would feel to a be unstuck, to have all of your wildest dreams comes true, and the be exactly where you want to be. How does it feel, in your body, your heart, your mental clarity, your inner peace?

Go through these questions as often as needed, to keep yourself moving forward, taking action, making decisions, and starting before you're ready. There are a million reasons why I shouldn't have gone to beauty school, twice, trained as a bodybuilder, had a child when I did, opened a salon, sold my salon, shifted my entire business and brand while the world was coping with a pandemic, started a podcast, written a book, the list goes on. But I did, and I regret nothing. Every little action I've taken has moved me towards the woman, the mom, the friend, the mentor, the colleague, and the badass coach I am today!

Remember, a little fear is healthy, it means you really care about something, and trust your intuition. Our higher selves know what's going on, and what comes next. It's up to us to listen, have faith, and take action.

When we lack

clarity

We lack

confidence

But Wait, There's More!

Love everything you've read, but want more? Included here are some of the specific Beauty Inspires Beauty podcast episodes (as well as the date they were released) that relate back to the chapters included within these pages. With over 100 episodes currently available to stream online, and 3+ episodes being added weekly, be sure to follow the Beauty Inspires Beauty podcast so you don't miss out.

Don't Let Fear Hold You Back – June 3, 2022

How to Trust & Listen to Your Intuition – April 22, 2022

5 Questions to Ask Yourself NOW – February 2, 2022

Boundaries, Hormones & ALL the Things – January 21, 2022

Starting Scared & The F Word – April 27, 2022

Ready is a Lie – June 10, 2022

Building Community – February 23, 2022

Creating Community – February 11, 2022

How Bad Do You Want It? – June 22, 2022

3 Mindset Hacks to Shift Your Energy – March 23, 2022

Indecisiveness is The Dream Killer – June 2021

How to Start Your Own Podcast – July 6, 2022

Feeling Stuck or Indecisive? – April 15, 2022

Jessica Burgio

About the Author

Jessica Burgio is a Brand & Business Mentor, Host of The Beauty Inspires Beauty Podcast, Founder of the Beauty Insiders Membership, Owner & Founder of Creative House SD Event Space in San Diego, California.

After spending nearly 22 years behind the chair as a professional hairdresser, Jessica never imagined she'd be stepping away from the salon but after discovering an innate passion and expertise for empowering creative, accidental entrepreneurs & beauty professionals to take control of their lives by building their own personal brand, she knew it was time for a change.

Jessica has won a gold medal for body building, built and sold two successful businesses, created a top-rated beauty podcast, been featured in STRONG FITNESS magazine, and painted the faces of some of the highest-level speakers and cover models around. Her love for people is unmatched. Making people feel beautiful inside and out is what drives her to keep showing up and creating powerful content. To not only motivate and inspire you, but to make sure you <u>know</u> there's a seat at the table for you if you want it.

Jess's unique approach focuses on supporting and encouraging her clients to grow through personal development & self-care, all while offering the tools and strategies needed to build a thriving, sustainable brand that stands out.

Through her podcast, networking events and in person workshops- she mentors creative entrepreneurs with concrete, approachable, and proven steps to help grow and scale their brand. The BEAUTY INSPIRES BEAUTY community was created simply to help creatives and stylists not only grow their business, but grow their confidence. She has a passion to teach, mentor and coach and believes when you truly step into your passion and purpose, everything in life becomes possible.

For more free resources, information about Jess, the podcast, membership, and how you can work with her 1:1, visit her website — www.jessicaburgio.com. And be sure to follow her on IG - @jessicaburgio & @beautyinspiresbeautypodcast

About the Podcast

The Beauty Inspires Beauty podcast is a must-listen show for all beauty professionals & accidental entrepreneurs looking to level-up their business & their life. Join host Jessica Burgio—former salon owner turned, educator & seasoned six-figure stylist with 20 years behind the chair—as she brings you the mentorship, resources, online marketing, must have tools & seasoned advice to pursue and most importantly, sustain, the career you've been dreaming of.

Be sure to follow & subscribe to the Beauty Inspires Beauty Podcast on your favorite streaming platform or at www.jessicaburgio.com/podcast

About the Membership

The Beauty Insiders Membership is an exclusive, members-only, hangout designed with YOU in mind. Filled with golden nuggets learned over 20+ years, through the process of nurturing a crazy idea into a thriving community, organizing sold-out events, hosting a top-ranked podcast & building six-figure businesses with a wing & a prayer, the Beauty Insiders Membership is a place for YOU to share your journey as well.

For more information & to claim your seat at the table, visit — www.jessicaburgio.com/membership